THE TEACHING OF THE QUAIL

The Christian poetry of
JASON HORSLER

Dedicated to my wife (Proverbs 31:10-31)
& children (Psalm 127:3)
- my earthly joy.

CONTENTS

FOREWORD

The poems in this collection represent the first 30 years of the best of my Christian poetry and are presented here chronologically. Join me on social media for notifications and fresh poems, or to let me know what you think of my work.

This book is one of a set of two. If you enjoyed it, please seek out my other book: *'Beware the Cheshire Cat '*.

RED HEMISPHERE

   The rusty sky reflects these leaves,
kicked by the wind and torn by season.
They've seen a better, warmer day,
fallen from the crown as death frees them.

   I pull my coat to my face - a shield.
The wind has drawn a sword to shave me.
The too keen winter chases this day.
I miss the heat that summer gave me.

   But in this time of green to red,
of lazy suns and rainy grey,
the wood just sleeps - it is not dead,
so in the park I kneel and pray,
in leaf-smoke incensed air.
   Praise God for an Autumn day.

WATCHFIRE

The warm sun caresses the frosted face -
that has long kept watch in the winter night -
with a light that feels like a summer's love,
though the season has passed as day to night.
How treacherous the promise of lasting heat
that is made at the break of the awaited day,
but the noon always comes and the sun soon sets;
our hopes are broken as the blue skies grey.
In the coming dark, cold armies of fear
besiege in their ranks and our watch must be set:
first, second, third, fourth, but none sleep with ease -
for who rests in such coldness
    and yet...

There is a light that shines outside of time,
in spite of days, years and ice-ages;
a warmth that burns in the cold without fuel,
without flicker, though the storm about rages.
We shall not wait for the slow coming dawn.
We shall not cry in the night when its cold -
not stumble, not fear, but sleep in sure peace
when the warmth of the light of the Lord
    makes us bold.

GABBATHA

And did He really stand,
                    before those traitors and the triers
and silently reign in peace and pain
                    over all His crucifiers?

They said He was a blasphemer
                              to fill the crowds with fury.
They said He claimed to be a king
                    to sway the Roman jury.

And yet, in mock reverence they crowned Him
                    and draped a purple robe around Him.

They did all this and washed their hands
                              with the gore of whip and rod,
while He stood on trial before them
                    and they stood on trial before God.

STONES AND PALMS

'Cry out stones!' sang the palms,
'for these, our bearers, cannot shout
the hail of the creator King
as He turns their logic out;
like a rudder the size of a hand,
upon a ship on eternity's ocean,
that achieves an impossible steering
and defies inertial motion.'

'Wave!' the stones replied,
'for we are too heavy to dance,
and though we live ten thousand lives,
this season's leaf has chance,
to suffer the donkey's footsteps
and play a susurration.
In this short time that binds all times,
let us aid His coronation.'

THE JUDGEMENT OF THE FIG

A man had a fig tree planted in his yard,
A man who loved his land and worked it very hard.
He sowed upon the right time
And reaped the grain grown tall.
For years around the fig tree,
the crops would rise and fall.

One day he went looking for his first ripe figs
And only found a handful, too rotten even for pigs.
So he took up a sharp axe.
'At least I'll have firewood,'
said he, 'it's wasting soil.
It's meagre crop - no good.'

But his servant begged him for one more season
and his master consented for the servant pleased him.
So that servant gave it water
And furnished with mulch the tree,
And, after that time of love,
what shall *your* harvest be?

TWIN

How can two be in one body?
The one worn at the knee,
with tear-washed face
and loved and free,
the other stubborn lustful,
with black glittering eye,
passing the first by,
yet both are me.

Do we share the dark one's guilt?
Here now the sinner prays,
then the prayer sins:
a life of nights and days.
There is no peace here.
In place of unity -
low duality.
Black and white make grey.

Which habit will consume me,
The pure or the dying?
One always full of joy,
the other, crying.
Yet Christ sees just one here
And shines the revelation:
We rest in his salvation,
and both keep on trying.

THREE OF TIME'S FOOLS

Who dreams of gold from lead or blood from stone?
What fool stares at the sun praying for shade?
Who reaches among thorns for fruit
or believes almighty a thing they made?

He who makes gods in his time.

Who weeps beside the great river,
thirsting over the smallness of their cup?
Who starves while among the harvest trees,
searching the horizon but never looking up?

He who believes this is all in his time.

Who is like the mouse nesting in the summer fireplace
or the traveller navigating by the cloud wrack?
Who runs with assurance of victory in the race,
setting a pace without knowing the length of the track?

He who places his hope in this time.

THE DESERT HAS GOD

Woe to you unleavened youth,
where is the yeast of experience?
You so quickly escaped oppression so fast
that you went into wastelands unprepared?
Now you cry for manna and meat;
now you strike the dry rock.
Soon you will ask the seas for a path
and follow pillars of fire
as far as smoke wreathed mountains,
dreaming of rest and milk and honey
but the promised land is forty years away
and though the road is dry and hard:
                         The desert has God
                   The desert has God.

TACTICS

The savage army raised its shields and charged.
Many months had they honed their art and spears;
the hafts of which were polished like stone
by hardened hands and familiar years.
They knew the use of their weapons so well -
they could feel their commander's coming calls.
Their lives had gyred upon this moment
when they ran screaming at the enemy's walls -
which bristled of a sudden with gleaming muzzles,
roaring to life in a bank of smoke.
The treacherous air buzzed and slew
and the proud wave of warriors bled and broke.
Ready as they were in their own form of war,
they were not prepared for what the enemy had in store …
Know the devil's tools.

WHY DIDN'T YOU GO TO THE MOUNTAINS, LOT?

Why didn't you go to the mountains, Lot?
The Lord commanded you so.
He spared you from sulphur, fire and salt,
yet still you would not go.

What did you fear in the mountains, Lot,
that was worse than wrathful rain?
He singled you out for salvation -
did you doubt He would do it again?

Why did you flee to the village, Lot,
to gather provisions and wine?
Would He abandon you to starve in the hills?
Would you limit his love divine?

Were you consumed with grief, o Lot,
blind to your daughters' need?
Abraham was near - you knew it, Lot -
your good friend's sons had seed.

Why did you settle for a cave, Lot,
for a legacy of shame and derision?
All because you limited God's great love
and doubted his on-going provision.

Why didn't you go to the mountains, Lot?
The Lord commanded you so.
May we all learn from your mistake, o Lot,
and go when God says *go*.

I AM GOMER

I am Gomer.
I wish I was not -
Self-serving as Sampson,
disobedient as Lot.
I am David,
staring from the rooftop.
Lying like Abraham,
why won't I stop?

I wish I was Daniel,
Nathan or Paul,
but they too had thorns,
flesh were they all.
Oh Jesus - My Hosea -
Forgive me - draw me near.

PRAYER

I have nothing to give
that you do not already own.
I have no new information
that you have not known.
What can I say
that would change your mind?
What or where can I hide
that you cannot find?
How can this creature
come face to face
with the Lord - the Redeemer -
so generous in grace?
Only you Lord, you draw me,
keep me and restore me.
What foe can have victory
with you fighting for me?

REAP GOD'S LOVE

When last did you plough this ground
walked over on the way to other fields,
disregarded beyond mere fallow,
a pavement that neither fruits nor yields?

Break it up, though it even blunts the plough.
Sprinkle it with water and with blood.
Forget the harvest you last planted;
sow afresh in this new mud.

Sow seeds that are right -
Sow a righteous seed
for it is time to seek the LORD,
until he comes with the rains you need.

And then you will gather
the neglected harvest from above,
for He who stands fast is unfailing
Reap God's love.
Reap God's love.

WHAT A FATHER IS OUR FATHER

What a Father is our Father,
who reigns from Heaven high above?
What a joy to be his children,
adopted in his lasting love?

Oh, what foolishness to tarry.
Oh, what makes a person stall,
when eternal life is offered
freely to us one and all?

We were once such wayward sinners,
sons of Adam and of wrath;
idol makers and deniers,
walking blindly on hell's path.

But the Father drew us to Him
who died for us upon the cross.
Perfect is His Son's foundation,
none who build there suffer loss.

What a Father is our Father,
who gave His only precious son?
So all who put their faith in Jesus
will boldly say: 'amen Lord, come!'

Oh, we know we will not perish,
for our God is all in all.
We will serve His great commission
until we hear God's trumpet call.

THE SONG ABOUT EVERYTHING

Whenever someone says there is no God
Or that at bottom there is nothing but pitiless indifference.
Yet you can't help but wonder because of wonder
If another explanation for everything would make more sense …

Just remember that the universe and everything that is
could not have come from something that is not
Nothing gives you nothing and nothing isn't anything
and everything that is, is quite a lot.

To say that one day nothing decided to become
in a flash of light everything we see
is quite absurd but I know I've heard
people say that they believe this fantasy.

We know the big bang happened - the science is quite clear -
but it doesn't much give us a valid cause;
not to mention all the detail and ratios bound up
in the constants and universal laws,

like gravity if it were just a smidge - a tiny bit -
too weak or, even worse, a little strong
then hydrogen forever or black holes everywhere
would stop me from writing you this song.

So who kicked off the universe and set it straight and narrow?
Please don't say nothing anymore.
Someone powerful and good - wise beyond all measure -
you can call him Jesus, God or even Lord.

Outside time and space - transcendent and almighty -
it is written that he said: 'let there be…'

Then light became apparent - and everything else was next my
friend
and I believe that that includes you and me.

─────────────────────── 𝒥𝒷 ───────────────────────

The luthier saws wood.
Offcuts fall and will be burned -
the guitar is saved

PEARL

As the swine disregards the pearl
and blithely chews the stale corn,
man can do no better
and is blind to truth, until reborn.
What can be seen through a fish's scales?
Even the mud of Christ is clear.
That which is whispered in the storm,
may He grant us an ear to hear.
For at best we are walking trees,
oh, the Bethsaida man said it true.
We cry "free-will" and shake our chains,
old wine-skins wanting new.
A passing thought, a morning mist,
calling supernature a delusion,
but the emptiness of matter and space
make our world an electric illusion.
"Time," men opine, "goes forever on -
live today for tomorrow we die.
The fife is played, the dirge is sung
and we, the market children, cry."
Shrewd as snakes, but without the dove:
a generation of dry bones lying,
thinking not of the Maker or Redeemer,
too busy living to see the dying.
And the swine still ignores the pearl;
the prodigal son desires the pods.
The Day of the Lord approaches swiftly, yet
the world wants lesser gods.

SAVIOUR

Thank you God - but I've got it from here.
You've set the course - now let me steer.
You saved me, yes, I know that story,
but here let me grasp some of the glory -
and so say that I have also saved
my worthy self from the grave.
And then I won't owe you my all
because I stood up from the Fall.
You can save me almost all the way,
just let *me* step into Judgement Day,
because your creature must be free
and I must owe some of Heaven to me…
    … *says the fool.*

Oh, my sin and weakness make my spirit groan.
You, Lord, must save me - and you alone…
    … *says the child of God.*

NOT MY HOME

I'm camping here and my tent is strong;
though no tent ever lasts for long -
> but this is not my home.

The zip may jam, the canvas sags.
The wind has ripped some parts to rags -
> but this is not my home.

The seams leak, the ropes fray,
the tarp tears and pegs give way -
> but this is not my home.

I expect the storm and the bleaching sun.
I know *I AM* - I am not alone
and my wearing tabernacle sighs -
> but this is *not* my home.

EVERGREEN

The leaf remembers when it was green
and the length of warmer days -
when it clung with ease to its twig
and glistened and flashed in the sun's bright rays.
Now it senses the fall
and the call of the forest floor.
It blushes red, then pitted and brown
and soon it is no more.
How long is the life of every man
from bud to the hungry mud?
Joy and sorrow for a few short seasons
and then to the Judgement of God.
Ripped and tugged by autumn breezes,
our evergreen hope is found solely in Jesus.

DROWNING GARDEN

In the final week they still swept their floors.
A gate was mended on the third last day -
the people in the village so stuck in their way,
that some, in leaving, even locked their doors;
as if to keep back the dam tide -
frail wooden levees that will not hold.
They die hard: the habits of old,
and cannot be casually cast aside.

There is a nephilim here, in the leafy dark,
staking his plants and pulling out weeds,
though the distant coffer dam is broken.
As in the days of Noah and his ark,
the gardener labours in vain for vain needs,
ignoring the government prophecy spoken.

SUSPECTED MASTERPIECE

A corner was all that remained of the painting
- a luminous lily with its shadow on the pond below.
No-one cared enough to pay for an appraisal.
Who could cash in on a mere fragment? So none now would know...
if the fire's victim that day
had actually owned a Monet.

He'd found it as an old man, stored deep in his loft.
Of a sudden everyone in the neighbourhood was his friend -
though behind their hands they all whispered with some glee:
"What if it was stolen or was a counterfeit in the end?
He is most to be pitied, they say,
if it is not a true Monet.

What will he do with all the money from the sale?"
What generosities owed and impatiently expected?
All had jealous motive and opportunity
None were accused by the police because all were suspected.
And he was most despised in that way,
because it was a true Monet.

WHO DARES ROUSE LEVIATHAN?

Who dares rouse Leviathan,
the Giant beneath the heaving deeps?
This world now teams with Ahabs
whose heaping anger never sleeps.
Each one wants to hook its jaw
and each to press its tongue;
to try its rich and fragrant oil
and see it bound and beached and dumb.

Poor soul captains on fragile ships,
vainly sharpening the barbless spear.
The Whale scoffs beneath the waves,
rising to teach all wisdom through fear.

Soon the Brute will breach and blow
and send each Pequod down below.

DISCERNMENT

The sandwich had a single grain of sand which
broke my uncle's tooth during lunch by the shore.
What the child then dismissed occurs to me now:
tiny contaminations hold at their core
secret destruction and misery;
life-changing, long-lasting - the gap in uncle's grin.
Such a small thing shattered the day
like a bulk of protein with a trace of poison
that kills the rodent. The gift of discernment -
the knowing of right from almost right -
to be aware when there is more than egg and cress
between the bread before the bite.

THE FATHER OF LIGHT

I walk before the face of the Father of light,
my feet in the dust and my new heart made right.
I feel his love, but I am wretched too
for the evil acts I would not, those I do;
and too often I leave the good things undone.
How can a saint and a sinner be one?
Shamed and contrite, I own my transgressions.
I sense His great gaze and make weak confessions.
What a dreadful weight - I fill with despair -
then the Holy Spirit reminds me He's there.

Oh the Father of light, in the peace of His face,
is satisfied with his Son and pours forth His grace.
Oh the Father of light, whose gaze never ceases,
looks upon my poor walk and sees the footsteps of Jesus.

WHEN THE MASTER RETURNS

A constellation of tools on the bench,
wood shavings curl and reach for the floor.
Rulers and callipers speak of precision,
charts with neat figures tell of it more.
Oil and glue with none of it spilled -
a place for everything and each in its place,
including the craftsman, kneeling to bring
his workpiece close to his face.
See him now ... his sweat covered brow,
a grimace with eyes gleaming bright.
His tongue pokes out, then turns to a pout -
the scene, a Rockwell delight.
Oh, to be found in such industry
when the Master at last returns for me.

THE TEACHING OF THE QUAIL

Freedom and the bread of Heaven;
water from rock and a path through the sea;
all came at too great a cost it seems
and the rabble cried out, "alas if only...
If only we had died in the lands of Kemet
where we all sat around our pots of meat.
The Lord provides but where is the fish,
the melon and cucumber, onion and leek?
We know best what our flesh requires,
for near two months we've walked this land.
Our memory of the plagues and the lash has faded
for our hearts are hard and our food is bland.
Curse this *manna* - what is it?
We are so much more worthy of a better god.
Other nations have golden idols
yet all we have is this Moses and his rod."

Then the anger of the Lord burned against them -
for they were still slaves who weep and wail -
so He gave them what their hearts desired
and fed them for a month 'til they choked on quail.

IMMINENCE

Instruments steadily gathered the evidence:
a slight bulge on the flank and a swarm of micro-quakes.
Each indicator collected as on a high blown cornice
like light, unremarked, individual snowflakes.
But here was more danger than a mere avalanche.
Ocean floor driven into the mantle by subduction
had melted into magma, steam and gas;
now surging to the surface for imminent eruption.
The farm animals sensed it and bellowed in fear.
The wild birds fled in the rotten egg air.
On far off screens the numbers turned red
while the folk in the village remained unaware
and went about their toil as in Noah's day.
Inevitable found the present and too few ran away

CYPHER

The Bard speaks forth twice:
the fourth prime line.
Enola and Eudoria had theirs -
this is mine…
I will group it as the lines
of a haiku verse
and each group thusly cut
will then be reversed.
The line divides neatly
in its meaning to all;
simply stated or hidden
some will stumble and fall,
yet you, dear reader,
if you keenly bend your mind
and seek my message,
you will happily find -
obey this cypher
and then you'll do well
for...

1st of 3; 4th of 2; 2nd of 3;
3rd of 6; 13th of 139; 2nd of 102
1st of 21; 5th of 23; 1st of 21;
4th of 2; 1st of 23; 1st of 153
3rd of 151; 1st of 23; 1st of 21;
2nd of 3; 2nd of 102; 3rd of 6;
1st of 33; 3rd of 26; 5th of 23;
1st of 38; 1st of 24; 2nd of 3;
1st of 3; 1st of 3; 3rd of 6.

A MATTER OF DAYS

A week of days for Israel
to weep for the one they killed
and all the promises for Jacob
will be perfectly fulfilled.

It's two Lord's days since He went up
and He returns again:
the day that no-one knows -
is not an *if* but a certain *when*.

A day of joy - a marriage day,
foretold in the distant past
when the Groom will come to take away
with a shout and trumpet blast.

A day of wine, a day of bread,
a day for the bride to raise her head.
A day so soon I must be brief
and challenge any unbelief,
for time is short -
do not be caught
with double mind
and left behind.
Read the word.
Did you hear?
Listen
if you
have an ear...
do not be snared in the sorrow
for the Day could be tomorrow.

FORGET-ME-NOTS

Rank upon rank they stood -
monuments to persons unknown.
Some must have cost a purse in their day:
black and red granite and marble like bone,
but time's bitter rain scoured much away.

Now the names proudly etched long ago
are clogged with moss and chipped by frost -
some of the graves, mere worn blank stone.
Who weeps for anonymous, the details lost?
Eventually the dead are all alone.

Was this once an angel with wings and a trump?
Did iron once ring this small plot?
I wished for more detail than just a death date.
What's in a name if all else is forgot?
Such carved legacy seems a legacy late.

Forget-me-nots whither here
and bring Charles Spurgeon to mind:
"A good character is the best tombstone"
It matters how you loved those left behind
not in how you were buried, but in how you were known.

AHAB BECKONS

Covet not the heart wrought of steel,
for hardness of heart is a curse.
A ship made of wood is a flimsy thing,
though it may serve you well as a hearse.

Now a tender heart is so much better
than the jaw of an oar biting shark
and, for the want of a hundred years,
a coffin will serve as an ark.

The doubloon went down to the deeps,
unclaimed on the smitten mast,
while God will hear of Ishmael -
the orphan afloat on the vast.

And strapped to the side of his whale
Ahab's arm calls us all to follow.
A mouldy and over-salted death
proving his gesture was wicked and hollow.

TRANSCENDENCE

It's said rust never sleeps
and you'll never see lichen grow.
The gradual is relentless:
the swell of fruit or glacial flow.
The continents are moving
and the mountains wear to plain.
You may watch them your entire life
yet you will look in vain.

Did you ever catch the leader stroke
before a lightning flash
or glimpse the perfect symmetry
of a single raindrop splash?
Caught between the sweeps
of a bumblebee's bright wing,
the sunlight makes a rainbow -
did you ever mark this thing?

Somethings are far too fast to see
others too slow or vast to see.
Only the eye of God can be
unencumbered by relativity.
The creator knows no limits,
He makes and plays with time.
It's hard for us to comprehend,
who tread the causal line.

LINGUA NOVA

Babel undone
when we see the Son
the Church becomes one
in doctrine and tongue
Maranatha!

When the bride groom has come
new songs will be sung
of victory won
everafter...

———————————————— 𝓗𝓫 ————————————————

Taken for granted:
close the fridge, shut the front door -
one last time for all.

WICKEDNESS

Something there is that isn't there
and ignorance doesn't know:
is a hole a thing or not a thing
and what about the shadow?
Does hatred fit this category?
Can you do indifference?
If I said this of your beauty
would you grudge me with offence?
If absence craves a fondness
and contrast minds the gap,
will you fall within the nothing?
Oh how sinister the trap.

For evil is the hole in good
and leaves undone the things you should.

BEELZEBUB

Innocent boys running wild in Eden -
a fresh start without preacher or teacher;
to play, to eat, to swim and to shout,
to gladly express their full creature.
The conch rings out and calls them to meet
at the platform of pink granite stone,
but the rebel Adam is already there
for not all of them want to get home.

The signal fire is unkempt and smoulders
while Simon is taken for the beast.
Paradise burns and calls to the world
for the heart of man is released.
Expect the same near the Judgement Day
when God takes all the restraint away.

GOODBYE

There may not be time and later is nigh -
we used to think there would always be more:
a chance and several others behind it,
but that was in the days before…

Before the sickness and the war;
digital money and famine looming;
before Laodicea began to fall;
morality withering - ignorance blooming.
In diverse lands the ground is shaking;
Jacob surrounded by 'boldened foes;
A.I. is writing scripture
and these birth pangs look like death throes.

There may not be time and later is nigh -
from the poet at the end of the world:
    goodbye!

BEATITUDES

If you find yourself poor in spirit
and are numbered among the meek;
if you hunger and thirst for righteousness
and mourn for you are weak;

If you have a pure and merciful heart
and spread God's peace abroad,
yet others reject your efforts
and hate you for the Lord -

insulted, accused - as the prophets of old
your righteous walk despised -
then you are truly blessed dear one,
have you never realised?

The words preached by the Christ himself
on that ancient windswept hill,
describe the child of God
and hold further blessing still…

for yours will be the kingdom,
what profound inheritance,
to see God and be called His son
and this, no arrogance.

Because Jesus gave us hope
He repeated "for they will be..."
filled, comforted and given
God's dear, but free, mercy.

Until then endure in faith and love,
and walk in gratitudes,
recall inside your hopeful heart:
you are the beatitudes.

THE TIBERIAN BREAKFAST

Not for the first time did those fishermen of old
spend the whole night with nothing to show;
and same as before, the man on the shore
gave them aid and then they did know
that Christ was there and Peter got wet
and this time, though full,
          they did not break their net.

Yes big Simon once more climbed out of the boat
and failed to walk on the water again,
but he'd only an eye for his blessed rabbi,
caring not for doubt, ridicule nor pain.
And though much of his error is spoken
note his desire to see God
          though heart-broken.

They had grilled the fare on Chist's coal flames
and the same kind of fire one night:
when Peter denied - then he and cock cried
and the sheep were all scattered in fright -
these same two fires burned the costly charcoal
that flame for evil and this one…
          for the good of a soul.

They all ate a breakfast of loaves and fish
to remind them of the multitude on a nearby hill;
and the catch final count was an exact amount
for 'not one shall be lost' was God's will.
They had added their fish to the work of the Lord
while Jesus showed Simon
          how he was restored.

IMPRECATION I

Scoffers - we note well your flash-mob clamour.
Your world-wide choir mocking what it doesn't know,
discarding tools of reason for the repeating hammer -
Goebbels' lesson rings with each dull blow.
Your songs in iron prove the prophetic scripture true:
in the last days the great delusion will fall
and all the things written will happen to you,
yet still you will curse the Gospel's call.
You blame anything, especially the people of the Lord.
You excuse everything, except the worship of the Lamb.
You are a house divided but in this you are of one accord:
using the lowest terms for the highest great 'I AM'.

God send the plague of thirty inch hail upon their error.
May your Kingdom come, will be done and the world perish in terror.

IMPRECATION II

Apostates - we note well your going out.
You swim the Tiber river and beckon us to follow.
Your leaving leaves us with little doubt:
the washed pig returns to its filthy wallow.
Your falling away proves the scripture true:
in the last days the great delusion will come
and all the things written will happen to you,
yet still you reject the finished work done.
You prostate yourself to the east - to the sun
and make the unversed into offspring of hell;
feeding them thorns and, just as a yeast,
you "angels of light" must poison each well.

God send them to outer darkness and unending fire.
Destroy the self deceiver and rocky ground liar.

THE CHOICE NOT TAKEN

Two roads diverged as they often do
and at the fork a skeleton lay -
a traveller who stood and thought it through;
as around his feet the bindweed grew.
He stayed too long to choose a way

Seeing both paths equal - foul or fair -
I wonder how his thinking went
that had him starved and rooted there;
caught in vacillation's snare
until his life was vainly spent.

We may say this fool deserved to die;
this ignoramus had no wit,
but for God's grace stay you or I
who do not lack the Lord's supply;
for decision has faith at the soul of it.

I shall be singing this by and by
somewhere many ages hence:
two roads diverged and it was *not* I
who made no choice except to die
and thus show God indifference.

HANDS DOWN (THE LENGTHS DEMANDED)

Two men decided to build a house
yet they lacked a ruler between them,
nor any type of measuring unit.
They fretted until they agreed then
to use their hands and digits
to cut wood and locate each wall;
and herein lived the problem -
for one man was short and the other tall.
Both started working on different ends
but their hands matched up with their height
and when they met at last in the middle,
the house didn't look quite right.
For one roof was halfway higher
and the other, halfway too low;
the rooms on the tall side, wide
and the ones on the short side, narrow.
When we judge ourselves by ourselves
our findings cannot stand.
When we do what is right in our sight,
we are builders building on sand.
And who wants to be shamed by the tower
they were never able to complete -
a monument for all to see,
to the fool without metres or feet.
We need a more sure measurement.
We need an unchangeable guide.
One who says what stands or falls
and which way is narrow or wide.
There are always twelve inches in a foot.
Oh I wish I could give them a hand -
our two fictitious builders
who need to understand,
there is a benchmark on creation

and perfection is the standard.
The Master declared it is finished,
who set and met the lengths demanded.

Time is like a fuse:
bright sparks crackle down the thread;
the powder is near.

MUD BABIES

Every saint is a baby, left in the mud;
abandoned and helpless, covered in blood;
useless, crying and close to our dying;
when God picked us up and said, 'you are mine'.

With our knowledge (or intimacy) of evil and good,
we presume the difference and do what we would.
No use in denying our imperfect trying,
reminded by scripture - we are *not* divine.

Therefore I express this fearsome perspective;
a more solid food as a timely corrective...
Can a baby advise the Father of Light?
The seer of all doesn't need infant sight.
Your life is a drop beside infinite seas
so come humbly to Christ on well-worn knees.

SPURGEON'S STARS

You cannot see stars in the daylight -
stars that guide where there is no track
and bring joy and hope in adversity,
proclaiming His work when the sky is black.
The night is full of danger and snares
but even the lowest wretch can peer
between the clouds to catch a glimpse
and sense the infinite drawing near.

Not so in the sun's benevolent glare
that prospers the garden and field;
though it paints the sky a joyous blue
while drawing up sap and ripening yield;
it also outshines the heavenly host,
blinding those who need the stars most.

HAPPY OBLIGATION

A Christian is one with Christ,
but what does one add to infinity?
If anything we feel we mar perfection
and detract from the Holy Trinity.

Ah, but Jesus can do what seems absurd:
impossible for man is possible for the Word.

He did things that only God can do:
He walked on water and calmed the wind.
He lead the life we never can
for, though sorely tempted, he never sinned.

He poured himself out and so must we
until we are utterly spent.
The only thing that we must do
that Jesus never did - is repent.

SPURGEON'S STORM

Becalmed in the doldrums, the sailing ships of old
were in far more danger there than in any storm or squall;
with a tinfoil sea and a weed thick hull;
meat would rot in the barrel when the glass refused to fall.

Men's bones grew weak and their teeth fell out.
Mutiny and madness boiled before the mast.
The weevils and rats despaired and died
for the hold was empty and the water wouldn't last.

Boredom plagued the minds of the best shipmates -
Pillars of old salt saw each other as food.
The lash would not contain them as the weeks turned into months.
The sunburnt skeletal crew became satanic brood.

Oh - we think we want calm, peace and idle time on deck,
but it is not the prayer-fulled whirlwind that makes of us a wreck.

EMPIRE OF DIRT

A mud city built in a slum
by a child upon his knees
replete with streets and tunnels
and a park with twigs for trees;
an old brick for the town hall
and tinfoil for the pond -
this little world so occupies
that he cannot see beyond
to the slime and litter around.
He keeps his young eyes down.

And his ears are likewise closed
for he chooses not to hear
the despair of adult voices
the anger and the fear.
Instead he whistles and tweets,
conjuring up a bird.
He growls an invisible car
and so doing he never heard
the offer of time at the beach,
for his grasp cannot exceed his reach.

TRIBULATION

How great the storm tugs at the anchor,
so deep the flukes bite the seafloor;
and as the wind tears at the rigging,
so tighten the knots all the more.
Some say it depends on the tempest,
but I say the chain, iron and rope -
for it is not disaster we measure,
but the means that gave us good hope.

So celebrate the life saving means
that helped you last weather the weather;
and do not begrudge the odd gale,
for no natural storm lasts forever;
and such times on foam pitching boards
will reveal the means are the Lord's.

CHRISTIAN GARDENER

Why do we still plant vegetables
and kneel to weed the ground
when all about the world
the end alarm bells sound?
Why do we prune the trees
and pile the compost heap
when half the lost are angry
and the other half asleep?
Why do we can and pickle
a harvest we won't eat
for soon we will be raptured
and before the bema seat?
So why stock up the freezer
with months of ready meals
when everything is pointing
to the tribulation seals?

I'll tell you why the Black Horseman
should make us do this labour
for though they ignore our warning
we can still try feed our neighbour…
*"Two pounds of wheat for a day's wages,
and six pounds of barley for the same work,
and do not damage the oil and the wine!"*

CHRISTOPHER'S CHALLENGE

Hitchens once said it was impossible -
it was a thing that could never be done:
to find a good and noble deed
unachievable without religion.

Yet this is hardly a challenge,
though I understand his strong insistence,
for the man lived to the end of his life
in denial of God's existence.

Yet it is a good and noble thing
to give glory to the Creator King
and this cannot be accomplished at all
without obeying the Gospel call
and thus belonging to the true religion
of the Bible-believing humble Christian.

WORSHIP

My fear of coasters vanished in an instant
when Lindiwe put her little brown hand in mine
and said, 'Mister H, please ride next to me.'
I recall it well in that far distant time -
my first school trip as a primary teacher
to Gold Reef City with my year five class;
and due to a trauma in my infancy
I had avoided such rides all the years in my past;
but that moment I looked in her wide wet eyes
I knew I had no choice but to go,
so we both bravely stood in the line with the others
and talked a great deal not to let our fear show.

We pointed out the solid welds and thick bolts
that held the track twisting in the sky;
the safety belts and strong guard bars,
the engineered what, the wherefore and why.
We agreed that thousands had ridden before us,
yet no-one was injured and no-one had died
and though they had screamed, those who came off
seemed by their faces to have enjoyed the ride.

Our turn came and went and all I can say
is Lindiwe and I rode many more times that day.

THE PRODIGAL FATHER

My father's voice booms around the house.
His heavy ring is on my thin finger.
His oversized coat covers my shame
and upon it his warmth and scents still linger.
The taste of pig pods are on my tongue -
a reminder of when I was at my least -
but soon it will be washed away with wine
and the fattened calf of my father's feast.
I see his servants rushing to prepare
and recall my resolve to be one of them,
but he refused to accept my works;
he called me 'found' and would not condemn.
I am his son and forever will be;
and forever remember … *He* ran out to *me*.

SATISFACTION

Hunger and thirst for righteousness?
Aye, this I do and more
(I fail so often and feel it
yet I want to obey His law)

But I starve for something else beside;
something guessed at and, for now, dim.
I want to know the elusive mystery…
I want to look upon Him.

To hear His voice and joy filled shout
and blast speculation with truth.
I desire this more than seeing loved ones
or eating His feast or eternal youth.

Satisfaction for my hunger is a promise
and He has perfected His part.
I know I will see my Saviour
for He has made me pure in heart.

TELL US AGAIN

Tell us again
about justification by faith alone,
for we are no different than Israel of old.
Each week we face Jordans and giants
as our memory dims - our faith grows cold -
and then we think we need to help
the Creator of all along;
as did Abram with Hagar.
We are blind, forgetful and wrong.

Tell us again
how a work and an idol can slip,
like a snake, in our adamic way.
We try to placate the impeccable
with some pitiful act or trite words we say;
when it's actually a contrite heart we need
to be humble in spirit and groan -
for his blood was and is all sufficient.
Tell us again
about justification by faith alone.

THE POTTERY SPEAKS

'We've been dug; we've been folded;
we've been fingered; we've been spun;
we were fired long ago;
we've been painted - we are done.'

But the prophet pot warned:
'Yes we have been here many days,
but we're still in the potting shed
and that isn't paint - it's unfired glaze.'

'Our creation might seem
to us to be complete,
yet around us the work doesn't cease.
A vase may dream:
the kiln is done with its heat
but we are not yet upon the mantelpiece.'

SORE

A notion must be tabled,
that always leaves me floored,
it is, though I am quite able,
I don't always fight my flaw.

Instead I seem to wallow in
those things against His law.
To be precise I speak of sin
that crucified my Lord.

My fleshy habits chafe me
and leave my conscience sore.
He alone must save me
and shape me with His Sword.

And thus lead me to knock and seek
As he stands beside a door
and smiles upon the humble-meek
declaring me adored.

KINTSUGI

I'm that cracked bowl lovingly restored to use.
Others would have called me worthless and old;
and discarded me at the very first sign of a chip,
but my maker and owner has glued me with gold.

So much had to be used that I am now twice as heavy,
and dozens of times more valuable, than new -
my crazed glaze and rim accented
with thick yellow metal against white and blue.

I am more beautiful now and held up to display.
My history gives glory to the one who restored me.
He purchased the gilt and with expert technique
met edge on to edge 'til I am unique.

He could have hidden his careful repair -
but then none would know the love he showed there.

LITTLE GREEN MEN

Today's alien is yesterday's fairy.
There has always been a need for capture,
for kidnap and trap and the taking of babes,
for a way to explain the rapture.

Today's alien is yesterday's fairy -
all the work of the prince of the airs,
who does not know the day or the hour,
but must always lay down ready snares.

Today's alien is yesterday's fairy,
filling up books and priming the mind,
manifesting for two thousand years
to cast doubt among those left behind.

Today's alien is yesterday's fairy
and if you don't have faith - be wary.

TO DO

Leisure has not been my friend.
What others treasure, I despise.
I'm inconsistent in my eyes,
but in the end I see a trend -
leisure's not my friend.

A challenge is what I need:
a job, a project, a drudge.
I burn clean at work, I judge.
When trapped in a task I'm freed -
a challenge is my need.

Satan loves an idle hand.
He always has, even at the Tree,
he saw the woman when she was free.
He'll stall me all he can -
he loves an idle hand.

I must find things to do.
To make, to bind, to paint, to write,
to create and all of hell to spite;
and in the doing I will stay true -
I must find things to do.

DOES MY GARDEN THRIVE?

Does my garden thrive,
   or do weeds now cover all,
to undo my most careful work
   before the trumpet call?

"Ay, the beds are tended
   and I have planted seed,
no change since you were caught up
   from the land you used to weed."

Do the Springboks still win
   at passing back the leather?
I cannot watch the Green and Gold
   now I am saved forever.

"Ay, the pigskin flies,
   though much of the team were taken.
They tried to keep their spirit up
   as the rest of us were shaken."

You know who I left behind -
   have they bought into the lie
that tries to explain our leaving
   in the twinkling of an eye?

"Ay, the ones you warned
   are reading your words now
and wishing they had listened when
   you said all knees would bow."

Is my friend believing,
   now I am in the sky
and does he still avoid the mark
   though he can't sell or buy?

65

"Yes, saint, I am abiding.
  I've read the Revelation.
I'll endure until God's altar calls
  and escape the beast's damnation."

Lay aside your load
The path and gate are narrow.
Enter in His rest.

EPHESIANS 6:12

From the bottom of the pyramid,
see the Punch and Judy show,
some are starting to call world governance,
is filled with bluff and blow.

From the cheap seats we can see
those who lord the stage aren't free...

Up with the hand or down with the wire -
shadow, sock or marionette -
what you watch may be human being
but also the devil's doing - don't forget.

He would have you asleep or laughing,
of that you may be certain,
but, as you watch the gaudy puppets jerk,
pay attention to behind the curtain.

ETERNALLY AND PERFECTLY

'Eternally' and 'perfectly' -
I say these words quite rapturously;
and sigh because both concepts leak
between my grasp so bound and weak
for who can claim such cleverness
as to understand foreverness;
and perfection is like a heavenly light -
can a shade of truth describe it right?

Yet I must at least in heart and head
hold the worlds of Jesus true.
The greatest sentence I have ever read:
"As the Father has loved me, so have I loved you."

So how has the Father loved the Son
And how in turn does He love me?
In quantity and quality?
Eternally and perfectly.

BE LIKE PETER

Peter leapt out of the boat by the seashore,
leaving his lifework behind him evermore.
Even the miracle catch couldn't hold him;
even the thought that the Lord might then scold him.
Left were his friends and his dignity also.
Grief and his love for the Lord all the more so
drove him through shallows, his wet robe about him;
eye on the Christ, he could not hear the shouting,
laughing or mocking of those by the nets;
letting his world go with no long regrets.
Perfect he was not, though love drove him on,
burned by betrayal, but wanting the Son.

I wrote this poem in a rare rhyming meter
all to say I want to be more like Peter.

PORTHCOTHAN

Porthcothan beach is narrow and long,
the sand is flat and cliff bound.
When the tide comes in, it comes apace,
and the unwary could be caught and drowned.

Near the low tide mark, a mother sunbathed
and building a castle by her toes, her waif.
I plucked up the courage to warn her that
the turn was coming and they were not safe.

But she frowned at my pleading, fearing no harm -
feeling was more important to her than being -
and besides to heed would disturb her lounge
and make necessary her packing and fleeing.

So she shook her fist, her voice a screech,
while I and mine retreated up the beach.

FREE

If you cannot see your lock what good is the Key?
A prisoner understands best the width to be free,
but what if the cage cannot easily be seen?
If a rope is unbreakable, does it matter if it's lean;
or the size of the knot, if it cannot be untied?
If you don't know the difference between in and outside,
does an open door make any sense at all?
And thus with the cross in the gospel call.
For who wants a saviour if they feel no threat
or redemption when they perceive no debt?
Does the unwitting slave want to be free?
In the land of the blind does anyone see?
This world makes real the warning so well -
the burn on the hand bears the hint of hell;
the pain in the gut tells of worms undying;
wrath and loss speak of gnashing and crying.
The curse in creation is a blessing too -
a warning that there is a problem with you.
The day of decision is always here,
but the last day to decide draws ever near;
and wisdom begins with the right kind of fear.
Do you think to earn eternity with a single life
and balance a tender future on that kind of knife;
where perfection is demanded and nothing less?
Only a fool puts forever on a guess.
But first you must know there is a scale
and a weighing time where most will fail.
You must know the chord of guilt that binds;
the lock that holds and the cage that blinds;
the rope and knot that hold you in -
you must know that you are bound by sin.
For if you sense that you are not free
perhaps you will seek and find the Key.

He is not far, He is ever here.
Call His name and He draws near -
the one they locked and caged and bound
and even buried underground.
Seek Him now - He will be found.
For He stood up and left their grave
and with that power He is eager to save.
Acknowledge your sin and your captive need
then the Son of God will set you free - free indeed.

Though the lame man walks,
proving his healer is God,
others shout 'sabbath'!

APLACE NOT APART

The store spaces empty.
  The lines grow long.
The weakened grow weary
  and outnumber the strong;
but don't lose your savour or heart:
  all's falling aplace not apart.

Where's the leader
  of church or state?
How few are the wise
  and less even, the great?
The end is yet merely the start:
  all's falling aplace not apart.

The light has turned off
  and the dim talk of war -
rumoured or atomic -
  as never before;
and make lying and fearing an art:
  all's falling aplace not apart.

The watchmen all warn
  of the prophecies spoken,
while hidden in the news
  the world's being broken;
the detail on an excellent chart:
  all's falling aplace not apart.

I plant up my garden
  and raise up my children.
I write so many poems
  to the world to warn them;
thus waiting, I'm playing my part:
  all's falling aplace not apart.

GREATER THINGS

I wonder if the caterpillar
senses its coming wings?
Does the breeze across the cabbages
tell the worm of flighty things?

Or does the little tadpole
have some clue its tail will go?
Does it dream of the coming hop?
Does it want its legs to grow?

I can only speak for myself -
and by a guess, for all mankind:
I have a mysterious yearning
for perfection in my mind.
We were made to be much greater
and we sense this may come later.

CERTAINTY

Something there is in the heart of man
that desires to see eternity,
to hate our death inevitable
and rage our ageing infirmity.
We dream of grails and fountains,
piling up great heaps of stone.
We bury much-needed treasure deep
and salt our flesh and bone.
Oh, the price we place on legacy
and the cost of religious pleas;
singing, praying and sacrifice,
wearing out our youthful knees.
We sense that death is wrong -
so much beauty marred by doom -
how can the glorious shining eye
become a socket in a tomb?
Yet we also cannot daily stand
to look down the unending hall,
and instead, peer blindly at our feet
as if our shadow was sum and all.
We seize the day, putting naught away
while the relentless forever waits
and time slips through our pinch
sealing everlasting fates;
but God has put in the heart of man
a desire to see eternity
and Jesus lived and died and rose
to give those He loves a certainty.

CONVICTUS

Out of the day that reveals me,
filthy as the pit in part and whole,
I thank the only God that sees
the need to rescue my cold soul.

In the fell steps of my fleshy dance
I have sought what is not allowed
and taken every sinful chance
and loved too little and seldom bowed.

I know beyond this place of tears
a time of light or a cage of shade
awaits for each in unnumbered years;
and this should leave the wise afraid.

The path is narrow and strait the gate.
So few find their name on the scroll.
I therefore pray Christ guards my fate
and I make Him captain of my soul.

RED HOT PENNY

Speculation is fit for predicting the weather
or any frivolous human endeavour,
but 'when it comes to how things eternally lie,
speculation is a red hot penny in the eye -
a painful loss of depth perception;
at best a guess or self-deception;
a grave misjudgement of the real;
a paper hope for a dreamed ideal.
A fool makes speculation stand
on opinion's ever shifting sand;
to build forever with a whimsical guess
and assume forgiveness - more or less.
The wise, however, seek to undergird
their hope on the sure rock of God's word.

EPITAPH (B.C.R.)

'Rest in peace' - the epitaph
that weighs as much as a last gasp.
R.I.P. is cheaper still,
applied in vain and vogue until
the meaning dies behind each word
and leaves the hope: cold and absurd.

But wake in agitation now
in angry heat and clear allow
this poet to sweep aside the lies
and say there is more than mere demise
for who is promised eternal rest
except those God has surely blessed?

All others remain at war with Him
and know no peace who die in sin.

The heavily laden who come to the Lord,
their stone may read: 'by Christ restored',
for they alone at death rest well.

Be warned there is no peace in hell.

NUMBERS

For your safety you cannot go there.
For your safety this is what you must wear.
You must restrict yourself for one more day.
You can think what you want but watch what you say.
Temporary powers and short term restrictions,
you'll get used to the new norm's piled interdictions.
These laws will pass by - or they will just pass
and all too many will dance on to the farce.
The unthinkable becomes the liveable;
the inexcusable becomes forgivable.
And as the cries of 'never again'
are misapplied or forgotten in the main
another crystal night looms incredibly
and blooms in the cry 'from the river to the sea'.
And all they need is for the good to be still
while letting the madness run forward with a will.
The new flag's much prettier than the old,
but will we learn from a history now growing cold?
Do we do what is easy and give evil a nod
and forget that these are the people of God?
      Who said:
Whoever blesses Israel will be blessed,
And whoever curses Israel will be cursed.

NO MORE

No more, the candle in the window.
No more, the marking on the walls.
No more marching on the highways.
No more meetings in beer halls.
No more strident voices emoting.
No more lines drawn on the land.
No more feeding of the cannon.
No more bleeding into sand.
No more apocalyptic horsemen.
No more death, nor sorrow, nor crying.
No more propaganda drumming.
No more ignorance and lying.
Never again, the pain of war -
when God at last declares: 'no more!'

VAIN ENDEAVOUR

They tried to poke holes in your bucket,
seeking to drain you dry,
for they are merely vessels;
self-contained within the lie.

The lie the serpent told
when offering Eve the fruit -
the secret in each heart;
deep and hidden like a root.

A root growing in the dark
which few will ever admit
that they can never fill
nor contain the infinite.

The infinite love with which
the repentant each are blessed,
who humbly know their limits
and whose sin has been confessed.

Confessed unto the Lord
who fills them up forever
and thwarts the one who drains
making vain that fool's endeavour.

Endeavour all they might -
and be sure that they will try -
they cannot but fail to empty
one who has the Lord's supply.

ESCAPEE

From the deep of my self-dug hole,
I can see the length of your arm;
and, though I wriggle and buck in your hand,
I can never despise your palm.

I am filthy from my digging
And exhausted from climbing in vain,
yet you wash me at your cost
and declare me without stain.

My excuses echo and haunt me -
my words sound like cheap old lies,
yet you never turn away from me.
You groan with me in my cries.

I will humble myself in your sight
but please Lord, humble me.
Keep in my mind how your reached and cleansed
and heard and blessed me free.

NEW EVERY MORNING

New every morning: the frost or the dew;
the hunger to break and the things I must do;
to stretch out stiff limbs and open the door.
New every morning - though all done before.

New every morning: the bird song; the light;
the work, the worry, the stand and the fight;
to face the challenge of earning my bread.
New every morning and closer to dead.

New every morning: my love for my kin.
On the mark, get set, go and set out to win;
feed them and clothe them - to send them out strong.
New every morning - my family's song.

New every morning: my prayer to the Lord;
to recall His promise and live as restored;
to trust in His blessing though all else may curse me.
New every morning - His forgiveness and mercy.

SURVEY

As I lie down to sleep, I take a survey
of all that I did, thought and said that day;
and wish it were different in many a way.
My short-comings drive me to humbly pray.

As I lie down and speak in the night,
I cannot sweet-talk the Father of Light,
who sees all my sin and how weak, my fight;
none-the-less, in His mercy, He declares me right.

As I rest at last in the peace of His grace,
I drift in bliss for I know my place
and, though each day is before His face,
He washes my sin and leaves no trace.

As I lie down to sleep, I take a survey
and marvel at God's loving kindness that day.

HE CAME

Would you look for God on earth?
What palace or mountain height
would be the place of seeking -
what stage of glory and might?

And who would He be with:
Poet, philosopher or king?
Who would God send forth,
ruling and proclaiming?

But no, He shames the wise
and has heard the powerless cries.

Would you look for God on earth?
The last place you'd look: a manger;
or worse a cross and among the lost -
for our Creator is no far stranger.

KING

When I belonged to myself,
at least when so I thought,
I did not value my things
and sold my pieces short;
yet also crowned myself as king
and wore that cardboard gilt.
My crimson robe was tattered
and as for the 'palace' I built…
It had a sand foundation
and the shame of half-made towers.
Oh, I leaned on my own wisdom,
trusting my imagined powers.

When I belonged to myself,
at least when so I thought,
I did not know that I am owned
and by whom I had been bought.
I have gladly lost my kingdom
and cast my crown aside,
for it was all a walking death;
now I step with Him who died.
My old life always ending
is now His life never done.
He declares we belong to each other
and His love has made us one…

my King.

NO ORDINARY PEOPLE

Mortal Egypt is now mouldering bones;
a magnificent corpse of sun-cracked stones.
And where is Rome, with all her roads?
Her decadent marble decays and erodes.
Terracotta armies with mountain spanning walls,
yet even long-lived China now falls.
Country, culture and civilization -
how many lifespans measure a nation?
From the time it became to the time it is done
and who are we in comparison?
From one view we are but a passing mist -
just another name on a generation list
but beyond our death, our time goes on -
eternity makes short what now feels long.
Each history seems vast but the truth is that
compared to us it is the life of a gnat.
It appears protracted yet it is past,
while we are each starting what will always last.
No art of man exists forever -
eternity makes dust of human endeavour -
but we have just started (mark this well)
an infinite experience in Heaven or Hell.
And no-one is ordinary - no, not one.
We all outlast the moon and the sun.
Even the dullest will one day be
a creature of light or a monstrosity;
a glorified saint beyond angel fair
or a demonic corrupted living nightmare.
So consider how, though we outlast nations,
we are moving each other to these destinations…
How some share the gospel and others spread lies -

one person confirming what the other denies.
Every human you see throughout every day
will spend their forever in a good or bad way.
So have mercy and warn them and be to them tender
for each is everlasting in horror or splendour.

--------------------------------*Jb*--------------------------------

When I ponder God -
An ant stares at the ocean.
Knowledge tends to nil.

ROOTS

Though I cannot see my roots,
I am sure that they run deep
and I will honour my forebears
who are buried in their sleep.

Forgotten their days may be,
who pierced the soil beneath my tree
and I will never know their names
and they could not know me.

But by the sweat of many brows
they in turn raised up their young -
those obscure and branching tendrils
from which my own trunk sprung.

I suppose I could track back
some names and dates of death
yet unknown remains the leaves they held
between first and last drawn breath.

And if the Lord delays,
then I will root as they:
anonymous but a stay unto
some descendant's future day.

OF THE MASK AND THE MIRROR

People prefer the mask to the mirror -
to be seen as they wish to be;
a coat of grease; of kohl and talc;
a paper face that sets them free -

or so they believe.
As did mother Eve

and her Adam as they sewed their fig leaves
to cover what the ponds of Eden would show:
a magnificent pair and a pinnacle
of God's great creation, now brought low.

In the cool of the evening
they learned self deceiving.

And we have all mastered what they first declaimed
as we step into our own limelight -
our makeup melts and our costume slips,
we deny the reflection that sets us right.

Each foolishly brags
of the good of their rags.

How painful and glorious the light-wreathed mirror,
showing the brave their miserable heart.
Be bold then and ask the Lord for his Word
to show you your mask and tear it apart.

THE TREE FALL

If a tree falls in a forest
and no-one with an ear is around
does its crashing into the earth
even make a sound?
Oh, they say the air vibrates,
but without a mind's perception,
no sound will then be heard
but that is a deception.

Because there is a witness
for every single fall;
for every sound and sight
He sees and hears them all.
His eye is on the sparrow.
His ear is near the tree.
His mind can conscience all
because everywhere is He.

BANG ON (CONED)

It is easy to bomb a farm in the night -
no potato puts up a fight;
the corn has no ack-ack
and the pigs have no searchlight.
You aren't above the target
if you're not evading flack.

In the dark it's hard to tell
if your bullseye is down there,
but if they send up shell,
then you know you're where they care.
They will only fire their darts
when you're threatening their hearts.

The response from the ground depends
if the truth you drop offends.

CHANGE

From the moment we are born we must change:
master breathing, learn to suckle, then to speak;
be clean, obey; read, write and play
Every day taller - in all ways less weak.
Change your clothes. Change your bed.
Change the hair upon your head.
Change the rhyme -
even the time -
length of line.
Change.

Get a job and climb the ladder;
buy a home and fill it with kin.
Count the years - count the grey -
Count the wrinkles in your skin.
More loss than gain;
itch and pain;
energy drain.
Change.

Until it happens just once more
the ultimate change that dwarfs all before
and makes any further change too late.
Death sets us in a forever state:
Where there's famine or feast
And we are saint or beast
great or least.
No Change.

IF I HAD A MAGIC PAINTBRUSH

If I had a magic paintbrush
like the boy in that age-old tale;
and all I painted would appear
fair in form and sized to scale;
leaping off my hungry page,
tangible to have and hold,
would I paint me a giant gem
or some slippery bars of gold?
Would I brush within a fragrant wood,
a reclining mansion home -
with infinity pools and sunny rooms
beneath a stately pleasure-dome?
Oh, I could sigh and paint a world
to put envy into a king,
but the one thing I could never paint
is my life without its sin.

WHITEWASHED

I look within and it's not far I see…
the self-righteous me - the monstrosity;
the judge with the blind inward eye -
who crosses the road and leaves others to die;
who always has just one more straw
and a neon sign for every law
that's strangely dim for the ones *I* dare -
I wish it wasn't, but it's always there,
like a foe just below my mind skyline.
I claim a mercy that's privately mine.
I decry other's sin, but excuse my own,
letting no man wander, but prone to roam.
Oh, I seek a splinter through a log,
this pearly swine - this vomit dog.
I charge others cost, but bear no loss,
when I, again, must approach the cross.
Does He there let me fall just to carry me
and teach me yet again not to pharisee?

THE BRIGHT HOUSE

Says the despairing...
I crawled into the front door
and then fell out through the back;
out of the darkness and into the light,
then too soon back into the black.
Oh, how narrow the bright house was,
with its short and threadbare corridor -
dirty and scuffed by so many feet
that stumbled through there before.

Says the saint...
How sad to think that life is brief
and dark death is the end to all.
It wasn't a house you passed through.
It was merely an entrance hall
to a prison or palace that has no end.
Which you will go to? - that depends...

SELFISHNESS

Selfishness is a power so strong
that it may kill itself at length;
like an angry boa constricting a saw
and dying by the inch with all its strength.

It is an over-salted thirst
that consumes all there is to drink
until it gobbles even the bitter poison
for it cannot taste nor think.

It starts as a warming fire,
but it flashes to five alarms;
and burns the grasping hand that feeds;
smoke-blind to how it harms.

It taints love and scars life
in all ratios and scales.
In the end it has but one sure cure:
a cross and three crude nails.

TWO SHRIMP

Two shrimp observed a whale's approach.
Said the one: "this thing has soft skin.
It has no spines nor claws.
I will stay here and fight with him!"

The other shrimp said nothing,
and just swam out to the side,
for he'd seen the whale's size
and sought only to hitch a ride.

"Watch me now, as I catch him,"
cried the first, as he readied to fight.
At last the other gave warning:
"you are a mite before a might!"

But, focussing on his weapons,
the first refused to see.
The second caught onto the barnacled side
and stayed alive and free.

And the belligerent shrimp?
Nothing now remains of him,
while the humble one enjoys
a wild and ocean-spanning swim.

MONKEY, MONKEY, MONKEY

'Hear no evil' grew up,
the fallen monkey broken,
believed he was just good enough
to hear no evil spoken.

'See no evil' evolved
and the monkey would not budge,
believing that there is no God
for he didn't want a judge.

'Speak no evil' slept
and the monkey last in line,
refused to make his mind up.
He thought he had more time.

Monkey, monkey, monkey -
too good, no God, no haste -
Screwtape's favourite clients -
eternally disgraced.

LEARNING TO LIVE WITH A SOUND

Thin steel cable slapping a hundred metal masts -
   a random ting-a-ting in the marine windy night;
the trucks shifting gear as they navigate the pass -
   roaring and grinding down a road out of sight;
the traffic of planes, flying low on the flight path
   with white noise and squeal of turbine and jet;
the hiss of a thousand rushing car tyres
   as they cross the Millenium Bridge, wide and wet;
the hum of the fridge like the drone of the fish tank -
   on and off through the hours with gurgles and sighs;
the life saving word of the Bible street preacher -
   repeating the Gospel until one of you dies.

If you hear something often you will soon cease to listen -
   jarring at first, when not there, will you miss them?

THEN, ONLY THEN

When the moon and the sea
make their last tide together -
then, only then,
have we started forever.

When the final tree
grows one last ring -
then, only then,
does eternal begin.

When every great mountain
has risen and worn;
and every last thunder
has riven a storm;
and every last sunrise
has gilded the morn -

then, only then
... forever.

When the last lie is told
and the last sin is done -
then, only then,
has everlasting begun.

When every last word
has been written and read;
and every last poem
has been weepingly said;
and the saints filled with joy
and the damned filled with dread -

then, only then,
does time truly start;
when mind and matter
meet spirit and heart
...forever.

What is my value?
I am grafted on the King's vine.
He gifts me my worth.

WORD

Happening now…
As all the props and platforms
are tilted and kicked away;
as every foundation fails
and the sheltering walls all sway;
as every shelf is emptied
and price outstrips accounts;
as all the stockpiles dwindle
and what is owed still mounts;
as all the shields split apart
and each sword grows dull and bends;
as every plan proves futile
and all alliance ends;
as hope becomes a memory
and trust is foolish vain;
as knowledge falls into question
and light begins to wane -

until nothing is left that is sturdy
and no true truth is heard,
we at last will begin to value
God's unchanging living Word.

TWO BLINDNESSES

I can't see how you believe in God
if He never gave you eyes.
It amazes me that one born blind
would fail to realise
that if an all-powerful God exists,
then none would be born blind.
So either He isn't, or if He is,
He's indifferent and unkind.

Dear friend, I've heard the wicked world
and I'm glad that I do not see
the filth and death of all which falls;
in a strange way I am free;
and since eternity is long,
I've merely blinked at the start.
The first thing I see will be Him
who has opened the eyes of my heart.

Each of us has challenges -
the crosses we shortly bear.
The joys of our life point to Heaven;
the woes say we're not yet there;
and these warn us too of the darkness
that will soon come to those not saved.
I'd rather be me without sight
than be spiritually blind and depraved.

I AM LIVING WITH TWO FUTURES

I am living with two futures
and I find them curious things,
like a bird who dreams of fins
and a fish who senses wings.

My one tomorrow demands
I make another five year plan
where I work to pay my debts
and become an older man;
where I help my son and daughter
to step strongly into life
and I plant and build and save
and I bless and love my wife.

My other tomorrow will come
and end the first one someday,
when the Lord of Glory appears
to take the faithful away
to a future I cannot imagine
and thus I cannot plan.
I can only trust that instantly
I will become a perfect man.

I am living with two futures
and I find them curious things.
This fish will dream of flying
Until God gives him his wings.

JETHRO'S BELIEF

Jethro's faith did not depend
on seeing what Israel saw.
His love for Moses and trust in God -
he believed with nothing more.
He heard of plagues and a sundered sea;
of manna and quail; fire and smoke;
of shaking Sinai's mountain of Law
and water pouring from the rock that broke.

Reuel, the priest of Midian, marvelled
at his son-in-law's words of God's wise ways,
yet he then spoke for God to command delegation
to better serve the nation and Moses obeyed;
and is relieved by the advice he received
from one who didn't see but believed.

ABOUT THE POET

I was born in 1975 in a small town on the outskirts of Johannesburg in South Africa. I had an adventurous childhood filled with beauty and challenges. I began writing poetry as a form of self-expression in 1988, having been inspired by my English teacher at the time. I was fairly prolific in the early years, but unfortunately - or fortunately because, as I recall, the vast majority of them were awful - I lost this first poetry collection when I went to college. It was also about this time that I became a Christian. My early Christian poems were naïve as I had yet to learn much of theology and so I now keep these attempts for my own private amusement (or horror).

In 2001 I immigrated to the United Kingdom and spent a long time in London before recently moving to Runcorn near Liverpool. At the time of compiling this anthology I live with my wife and two children. We are a happy and blessed family. I am a musician specialising in drums and ukulele. I am also a teacher and an avid gardener and an occasional woodworker.

My main influences have been Frost, Blake, Owen, Shelly, Patten, Housman, Hughes, Wordsworth and Shakespeare; but I love good poetry wherever I find it and enjoy reading excellent verse from undiscovered, uncelebrated poets and lyricists. My favourite form is the sonnet - both to read and to write - because I like the brevity of it. A good poem should start a thought and then leave the reader time to think - and desiring more from the poet. I write a fair amount of haiku in order to, as I see it, "keep the pipes open". Capturing an idea in a strict seventeen syllable structure with some sort of imagery is a really good regular exercise for a poet. I have included a small collection of these haiku in this book where there is space at the end of short or very long poems.

It is my greatest hope that my poetry inspires others or better yet leads them to think more clearly and deeply about who they are and who God is - and perhaps, with that terrifying realisation, they might see the absolute necessity for faith in the finished work of Christ on the cross and that they might have peace in the love of God.

INDEX & NOTES

A Matter Of Days - (07/2023) *See Daniel 9; Zechariah 12:10; 2 Peter 3:8; Matthew 24:36; Acts 1:2; 2 Corinthians 11:2; Luke 21:28 & 2 Corinthians 6:2.*

Ahab Beckons - (07/2023) *See chapter 135 of Moby Dick by Herman Melville. Note that Captain Ahab has many deliberate associations with the evil God-hating Ahab of Kings 16:28–22:40.*

Aplace Not Apart - (10/2023) *See Ephesians 1:11; Isaiah 25:1; Romans 8:28.*

Bang On (Coned) - (01/2024) *'Bang on' a war time slang phrase meaning to be on target. 'Coned' means to be spotted in a search light and then pounded by flack. See John 15:20; 3:19; 8:34.*

Be Like Peter - (09/2023) *See John 21:1-13.*

Beatitudes - (07/2023) *See Matthew 5:2-12.*

Beelzebub - (07/2023) *Inspired by 'Lord of the Flies' the 1954 novel by William Golding. See also 2 Thessalonians 2:6–7.*

Certainty - (10/2023) *See Ecclesiastes 3:11; Luke 1:4; 2 Corinthians 5:1-10.*

Change - (01/2024) *See 1 Corinthians 15:51-52; 1 Thessalonians 4:17; Romans 8:19-21; 2 Corinthians 5:1; Revelation 21:5.*

Christian Gardener - (08/2023) *See Revelation 6:5-6.*

Christopher's Challenge - (08/2023) *Christopher Hitchens (1949 – 2011) was an author, journalist and popular outspoken atheist. See Hebrews 11:6-8.*

Convictus - (10/2023) *Written as an antitheses to 'Invictus' by William Ernest Henley, a poem that is distinctly contrary to the biblical Christian worldview. See Proverbs 9:10; Matthew 7:13-14; Revelation 3:5; 13:8; 20:12 & 15.*

Cypher - (07/2023) *Enola and Eudoria are characters in the cypher rich book series - 'Enola Holmes' by Nancy Springer.*

Discernment - (07/2023) *See 1 John 4:1; Matthew 7:15-16 & Hebrews 5:14.*

Does My Garden Thrive? - (09/2023) *Inspired by one of my favourite poems is Housman's: 'Is my team Ploughing?' - a classic which portrays a conversation between a dead man and his best friend - the deceased asking questions on the odd stanzas and the living answering them on the even stanzas. See 1 Corinthians 15:51-52; Romans 14:11; Philippians 2:10; 2 Corinthians 6:2.*

Drowning Garden - (06/2023) *Inspired by historic events such as Capel Celyn and Derwent village. See Matthew 24:37 & Luke 17:26 - 27.*

Empire Of Dirt - (08/2023) *Inspired by the C.S. Lewis quote: "it would seem that Our Lord finds our desires not too strong, but too weak…like an ignorant child who wants to go on making mud pies in a slum because he cannot imagine what is meant by the offer of a holiday at the sea. We are far too easily pleased." See 1 Corinthians 2:9; Isaiah 65:17 & James 1:12.*

Ephesians 6:12 - (09/2023) *See Revelation 13:1-18; 17:17; 2 Thessalonians 2:9; Daniel 12:10; 2 Corinthians 11:13-15.*

Epitaph (B.C.R.) - (11/2023) *See Matthew 11:28-30; Isaiah 57:2; Matthew 10:28; 25:46; John 3:18; 1 Thessalonians 4:13; Colossians 1:13-14.*

Escapee - (11/2023) *See Colossians 1:22; Hebrews 9:14; Romans 8:26-27; 1 Peter 5:6; John 8:36.*

Eternally And Perfectly - (09/2023) *See John 15:9; 17:23-26.*

Evergreen - (12/2022) *See James 4:14.*

Forget-Me-Nots - (07/2023) *Inspired by the Charles H. Spurgeon quote: "A good character is the best tombstone. Those who loved you and were helped by you will remember you when forget-me-nots have withered. Carve your name on hearts, not on marble."*

Free - (10/2023) *The second line is based on a quote from 'Les Miserables' by Victor Hugo. See Revelation 3:17; Ephesians 2:1; 2 Corinthians 6:2; Proverbs 9:10; Matthew 5:48; Acts 17:27; Psalm 69:32; Luke 11:9; John 8:36.*

Gabbatha - (02/2002) *The place of the trial of Jesus before his crucifixion. See John 19:13.*

Goodbye - (07/2023) *See Revelation 6; Revelation 3:14-22; 2 Timothy 3:1-13; 2 Thessalonians 2:11; Luke 21:11, 20-23 & Matthew 24:8.*

Greater Things - (10/2023) *See Matthew 5:48; Philippians 3:12; Philippians 1:21; 2 Corinthians 5:1-2.*

Hands Down (The Lengths Demanded) - (08/2023) *See Matthew 5:48; 2 Corinthians 10:12 & John 19:30.*

Happy Obligation - (08/2023) *See Acts 11:26; John 17:23; Mark 10:27; Hebrews 4:15; Numbers 23:19 & Matthew 16:24-26.*

He Came - (12/2023) *See Philippians 2:5-7; Hebrews 12:2; 1 Corinthians 1:27–31; Psalm 34:18; 85:9.*

I Am Gomer - (09/2016) *See Hosea 3.*

I Am Living With Two Futures - (03/2024) *See Philippians 1:21; 1 Timothy 5:8; Revelation 3:10; 1 Corinthians 15:52; 1 Thessalonians 4:16-17.*

If I Had A Magic Paintbrush - (01/2024) *The Magic Paintbrush is a popular Chinese folktale. 'Stately pleasure dome' is a direct reference to Xanadu in the poem 'Kubla Khan' by Samuel Taylor Coleridge. See Ephesians 2:8-9; Romans 3:20; Luke 18:27.*

Imminence - (07/2023) *See James 5:8; Revelation 1:3; 1 Corinthians 1:7; Luke 12:40; 1 Thessalonians 4:13-18 & 1 Corinthians 15:50-54.*

Imprecation I - (08/2023) *See Jude 1:17-20; 2 Peter 3:3-8; Proverbs 19:29; Proverbs 3:32-35; Galatians 6:7-8; Psalm 2 & Revelation 16:21.*

Imprecation II - (08/2023) *See 1 Timothy 4:1; 2 Timothy 4:3-4; Hebrews 3:12, 6:4-6, 10:26-29; Luke 8:13; 2 Peter 2:1, 17, 20-22; John 15:6 & 1 Timothy 4:1-2.*

Jethro's Belief - (04/2024) *See Exodus 18; John 20:29.*

King - (12/2023) *See Matthew 7:24-27; Luke 14:28-30; Proverbs 3:5-6; 1 Corinthians 7:23; Revelation 4:9-11; Ephesians 2:1; John 14:20.*

Kintsugi - (09/2023) *Kintsugi is a Japanese art of repairing a broken bowl or pot with lacquer and/or gold thus adding value to something which would normally be discarded. When Jesus rose from the dead, His glorified body still had the scars of his death (John 20:27) - and we see this in Revelation 5:6. I wonder if we too might have something to show in our glorified bodies of how much He did for us - to gladly give Him glory for His work in the eternal kingdom to come.*

Learning To Live With A Sound - (03/2024)

Lingua Nova - (07/2023) *See 1 John 3:2-3 & Revelation 22:12-20.*

Little Green Men - (09/2023) *See Ephesians 2:1–2; Matthew 24:36; 1 Peter 5:8.*

<u>Monkey, Monkey, Monkey</u> - (02/2024) *Screwtape is a reference to that excellent book by C. S. Lewis. See Romans 3:10-12; Psalm 14:1; John 3:36; Romans 1:18-20; 2 Corinthians 6:2; Daniel 12:2.*

<u>Mud Babies</u> - (08/2023) *See Ezekiel 16.*

<u>New Every Morning</u> - (11/2023) *See Lamentations 3:22-23 and Zephaniah 3:5.*

<u>No More</u> - (11/2023) *See Revelation 21:4; Isaiah 2:4; 25:8.*

<u>No Ordinary People</u> - (12/2023) *Inspired by a favourite C.S. Lewis quote: "It is a serious thing to live in a society of possible gods and goddesses, to remember that the dullest most uninteresting person you can talk to may one day be a creature which,if you saw it now, you would be strongly tempted to worship, or else a horror and a corruption such as you now meet, if at all, only in a nightmare. All day long we are, in some degree helping each other to one or the other of these destinations. It is in the light of these overwhelming possibilities, it is with the awe and the circumspection proper to them, that we should conduct all of our dealings with one another, all friendships, all loves, all play, all politics. There are no ordinary people. You have never talked to a mere mortal. Nations, cultures, arts, civilizations - these are mortal, and their life is to ours as the life of a gnat. But it is immortals whom we joke with, work with, marry, snub, and exploit - immortal horrors or everlasting splendours." (The Weight of Glory - 1949 MacMillan)*

<u>Not My Home</u> - (11/2022) *See 2 Corinthians 5:1-2 & Hebrews 13:14.*

<u>Numbers</u> - (11/2023) *See Numbers 24:9; Genesis 12:3.*

<u>Of The Mask And The Mirror</u> - (12/23) *See Genesis 3:7; Hebrews 4:12.*

<u>Pearl</u> - (10/2020) *See Matthew 7:6.*

<u>Porthcothan</u> - (09/2023) *See John 3:19; 15:20; Jeremiah 9:6; James 4:4; Joshua 24:15.*

Prayer - (10/2016) *See Psalm 50:10; Isaiah 40:13-14; Job 21:22; Jeremiah 23:23-24; Psalm 139:7-12 & Romans 8:31-33.*

Reap God's Love - (10/2016) *See Hosea 10:12.*

Red Hemisphere - (10/2001)

Red Hot Penny - (11/2023) *See Matthew 7:24-27; 2 Timothy 2:23; 2 Corinthians 10:5; 2 Peter 1:19; 3:15-16; 2 Timothy 3:16.*

Roots - (12/2023)

Satisfaction - (09/2023) *See Matthew 5:6; 5:8; Psalm 63:1.*

Saviour - (05/2022) *See Ephesians 2:8-9 & Romans 9:16.*

Selfishness - (02/2024) *See Philippians 2-11; Galatians 6:2; Hebrews 13:16.*

Sore - (09/2023) *See Romans 7:7-25; Ephesians 6:17; Revelation 3:20; Matthew 7:7.*

Spurgeon's Stars - (08/2023) *Inspired by Charles H. Spurgeon quote: "Hope itself is like a star - not to be seen in the sunshine of prosperity, and only to be discovered in the night of adversity"*

Spurgeon's Storm - (08/2023) *Inspired by Charles H. Spurgeon quote: "Storms afford the safest sailing for a Christian, calms are for him more terrible than whirlwinds."*

Stones And Palms - (04/2002) *See Luke 19:29–40 & John 12:12–19.*

Survey - (11/2023) *See Psalm 51:3-4; 38:9; 56:13; 139:1-10; Matthew 6:8; Hebrews 10:10.*

Suspected Masterpiece - (06/2023) *See John 15:18-25.*

Tactics - (06/2003) *See 'Precious Remedies Against Satan's Devices' by the puritan, Thomas Brooks.*

Tell Us Again - (09/2023) *See Romans 5:1; Galatians 3:24; Ephesians 2:8; Titus 3:5; Deuteronomy 1; Genesis 16; Psalm 51:17; Ephesians 1:7.*

The Bright House - (02/2024) *See James 4:14; 1:10; Psalm 39:5; Job 7:6-7; John 17:3.*

The Choice Not Taken - (08/2023) *See Acts 17:30; Romans 1:19-20; Acts 14:17 & Hebrews 1:1-3.*

The Desert Has God - (04/2003) *See Psalm 46:1; Ecclesiastes 7:14 & Deuteronomy 8:16.*

The Father Of Light - (07/2023) *See James 1:17; Psalm 56:13; Psalm 139:1–4, 7–10; John 13:10; Ezekiel 36:26; Romans 7; 1 John 1:9; Luke 9:35; Psalm 80:7; Numbers 6:24-26; Galatians 3:27; 2 Corinthians 5:21 & Colossians 3:3.*

The Judgement Of The Fig - (05/2002) *See Luke 13:6–9.*

The Pottery Speaks - (09/2023) *See 1 Peter 1:7; Malachi 3:3; Proverbs 25:4; Psalm 66:10; Isaiah 65:17; Romans 8:22; Revelation 21:5; 22:3; 1 Corinthians 15:52; Job 33:6; 2 Corinthians 4:7.*

The Prodigal Father - (09/2023) *See Luke 15:11-32.*

The Song About Everything - (09/2018) *Inspired by a Monty Python song. The first stanza is spoken, the rest is sung.*

The Teaching Of The Quail - (07/2023) *See Exodus 16 & Numbers 11.*

The Tiberian Breakfast - (08/2023) *See John 21.*

The Tree Fall - (12/2023) *See Jeremiah 23:23-24; Proverbs 15:3; Colossians 1:17; Psalm 139:7-10; 32:8; Matthew 6:6; 6:26; 10:29.*

Then, Only Then - (03/2024)

Three Of Time's Fools - (04/2003) *See Isaiah 40:18-20; 41:5-7; 22:13; Luke12:15-21,33-34 & 1 Corinthians 15:19.*

To Do - (09/2023) *English Proverb: 'the devil makes work for idle hands'. See 1 Timothy 5:12-13; 1 Thessalonians 4:11; 3:10-13; Ecclesiastes 9:10; Colossians 3:23; 1 Peter 5:8.*

Transcendence - (07/2023) *See 2 Chronicles 2:6; Isaiah 55:8-9; Jeremiah 23:23-24; 1 Kings 8:27; Matthew 10:29-31; Luke 12:7 & Romans 11:33-36.*

Tribulation - (08/2023) *Inspired by Charles H. Spurgeon quote: "The more the wind rages the more you feel that the anchor holds you."*

Twin - (01/2003) *See Romans 7:14-25 & Galatians 5:17.*

Two Blindnesses - (03/2024) *See Ephesians 1:18; Acts 26:18; Matthew 13:15-16; 16:24-26.*

Two Shrimp - (02/2024) *See Proverbs 1:7; 111:10; Proverbs 9:10; 2:4-5.*

Vain Endeavour - (11/2023) *See Romans 8:31-32; Psalm 118:6.*

Watchfire - (12/2001)

What A Father Is Our Father? - (01/2017) *A song to be sung to the tune of 'What A Friend We Have In Jesus' by Joseph M. Scriven.*

When The Master Returns - (07/2023) *See Hosea 10:12; Matthew 24:36,42-43, 25:1-13 ; 1 Corinthians 15:52; Mark 13:33-37; Luke 12:35-38; Romans 13:11; 1 Thessalonians 5:6 & Revelation 3:3.*

Whitewashed - (01/2024) *See Luke 10:25-37; 11:46; Matthew 7:5-6; 23:13-32; Proverbs 26:11.*

Who Dares Rouse Leviathan? - (06/2023) *See Job 3:8, 41:1; Psalm 2; Revelation 3:17; Hebrews 6:4-8; Proverbs 9:10 & chapter 36 of Moby Dick.*

Why Didn't You Go To The Mountains Lot? - (08/2013) *See Genesis 19.*

Wickedness - (07/2023) *See James 4:17; Luke 12:47; John 9:41; 2 Peter 2:21 & Romans 7:15.*

<u>Word</u> - (03/2024) *See 2 Peter 1:19.*

<u>Worship</u> - (08/2023) *See Psalm 100:1–5 & Psalm 40:3. Gold Reef City is a theme park in South Africa.*

———————————————— *Jh* ————————————————

Printed in Great Britain
by Amazon

41795235R00066